Cell Phone

HOW THINGS WORK

N Chokkan

Prodigy

Cell phone

First Edition: March 2010
80 Pages
Printed in India.

ISBN 978-81-8493-435-9
Pro-ya-en-77

Prodigy Books
177/103, First Floor, Ambal's Building
Lloyds Road, Royapettah, Chennai 600 014.
Ph: +91-44-4200-9603
Email: support@nhm.in
Website: www.nhm.in

Prodigy Books is an imprint of New Horizon Media Pvt. Ltd.

Contents

A Rectangular World

First things first, let us start with a flashback.

Don't worry, it won't take long; we can return home for dinner. Say 'bye' to your mom and dad, and get ready.

Ten years ago, almost all the houses had some curious looking notebooks, which they called the telephone book. People used it to note down names and phone numbers of their relatives and friends in perfect alphabetical order. Whenever they wanted to talk to somebody, all they needed to do is refer to this book and voila! They got the required phone number!

Surprisingly, now we don't find such notebooks anymore. Why? How can they all vanish all of a sudden?

For the past many years, technical experts have been predicting that our world is shrinking. Not physically, really. But each one of us is getting connected to all others, making it a global village.

As a sign of times, a tiny rectangular box called mobile phone or cell phone, has replaced all our address books and telephone diaries. If you have a tiny mobile phone on hand, you are connected to the entire world - whether it is the friend next door, or uncle in Singapore, or penguins in Antarctica, all you need to do is press a couple of buttons and the connection is established.

In fact, a mobile phone does much more than plain talking. You have a camera to take pictures of your memorable moments in life, organisers and calculators to help in everyday tasks and transactions; you can play games, listen to music, radio, video, live cricket scores; reserve train tickets, pay electricity bill, check your examination score and so on.

Our previous generation saw the revolution of a personal computer, which improved everyone's lives to a great extent. Now, mobile phones are revolutionising the world (and doing much more) for this generation.

A smart phone does everything that a personal computer does. Even the cheapest mobile phone can help in people's daily tasks, especially of those who do not have any computer awareness.

Most importantly, mobiles have a huge reach - you can see phones even in small cities and villages. From leaders, cinema personalities, sports stars and industrialists to farmers and illiterate workers, everyone seems to have a mobile phone (or two) on hand. This is because they cost much less compared to computers.

The fact is that most people of this generation can't live without a mobile phone. It has become a single window to the external world and a huge life saver, and can be compared to even oxygen.

You might have read science fiction, where machines take complete control of the world. When we read them, it looks like a very wild, funny imagination, to think of human beings becoming slaves of stupid machines.

But just look at what mobile phones are doing to us today. They have changed our life styles so much that they even determine what we should do at what time, who should talk to us and who shouldn't.

Today, we assume that a mobile phone is all we need to succeed in this world. Is there any truth in it? Is the growth of mobile phones and their impact good for the society? Or is it bad? Are there any side effects which we are overlooking?

Before we seek answers to these questions, let us see how this mobile revolution began. Who started it and where? Modern mobile phones are so small that we take them for granted. But was it like this from the very beginning? How did we arrive at this mobile generation, and where are we going from here? Answers to these questions could form a fascinating story!

The Story Of Wires

Let's start from the basics. When it comes to wireless, mobile telephony, the story actually starts with wires. Real hard, round, long wires which ran miles and miles.

You might see such telephone wires even today. But as we are so used to mobile phones, we don't notice them or care much about the wires.

However, for us to understand how the mobile telephones evolved, we need to know the story of phones in general, or what we call Land Line phones these days.

Earlier, all our phones were immobile. In other words, they would sit in one corner of the house and were tied by wires. People had to go near them to make or answer a call.

For a moment, let us imagine that we are removing the wires from these phones. What will happen next? We call such phones 'dead'. They will not (and cannot) work anymore. We can't call anyone using this phone, and nobody can call us too because the wires, the life of these phones, are now disconnected.

Of course, it's not a permanent damage. If we want to bring this phone back to life, all we need to do is connect the tiny wires again.

No one would disconnect a phone on purpose and kill it. But what if a rat chews on the wire? What if a child pulls the wire and cuts it by mistake? Because of such mishaps, we may lose the all-important communication line with the world.

Another problem is that you may have a land line phone at home, and another one at office. But what if you are caught between these two places? Again, nobody can contact you if there is an urgent message to be passed on.

For many years, scientists, inventors and industrialists set thinking about these problems and asked an important question 'Why do phones need wires? Can't we make a telephone without any wires? Won't it be nice to carry it wherever we go?'

Those days, this question sounded silly because wires were the most important part of a telephone. Removing them from the phone architecture looked like a stupid idea. People made fun of inventors pursuing this unlikely dream.

But luckily, the inventors didn't give up. They continued their research on wireless telephone technology. After a long struggle and many failures, they finally achieved success, which changed our world forever.

Wireless communication is not new to us. From ancient days, people have been talking to each other with the help of words, sign language etc., where we don't need any wires to say 'hello' or to discuss a very complex problem.

Then evolved exciting techniques like smoke signals, drum beat signals etc. which were used to send messages to people in distant places. Again, no wires were necessary and the communication spread in the air, like today's mobile phones.

Later, paper-like stationery was invented. You might have read stories of kings who wrote their secret instructions or letters in a scroll and sent them through messengers or carrier pigeons. This old but effective method was used even during the 20th Century (during World War I).

Spoken and written communications were some of the important factors which improved the human thought process. Till these modes of sharing information evolved, people acted like individual islands, and the concepts of society and community feeling were missing.

We are indebted to our carrier pigeons, which gave the idea for the evolution of a modern postal department. Now you can write a letter to anybody in the world, drop it in the nearest post box and it will reach them without any further effort from your side.

Today, this sounds ridiculously simple and obvious. But much earlier, it was a big advancement. The huge network of post offices across the globe was man's first communication revolution.

Sending letters through post was a great convenience and an excellent personal/business tool. It made people think in broader terms. People were no more afraid of travel, as they knew home was just a post card away. Also, they started doing business outside their own city, state and country as the presence of a postal network slowly eliminated such boundaries.

Slowly, man started thinking ahead. 'I write a letter to somebody. It takes couple of days, or sometimes a week to reach the person. And when the receiver writes a response, again it takes many days to reach me. Why should I wait for so long for a simple communication? Can something be done to speed this up?'

Another reason for this thought process was the urgency of messages. When somebody's building is on fire, we can't send a letter and wait for many days to get a response. Similarly, if you want to send birthday wishes to somebody, it may be too late by the time they get your letter.

Because of these reasons, people started thinking about a faster communication channel, which can be used in important and urgent situations. That's when the telegram was invented.

In 1837, Samuel Morse introduced this technology. Messages can be sent through a wire, and it would reach the destination in a matter of hours, instead of days. People were astonished at this wonder device, which made their communication so simple and swift.

Morse's technology is used even today. In fact, the method of sending different characters through telegram is named after him as Morse code in honor of this great inventor.

To understand Morse code, simply think of a dictionary. Look at this simplified example:

Pen = A writing instrument

Now you have a word ('pen') on the left side, and its meaning is specified on the other side. A dictionary has thousands of such word–meaning pairs to help us understand the language better. It acts as a learning tool when you are reading a book or a newspaper.

Morse code also has a similar structure. But here, instead of words, we have characters and special signs. For Example:

A = .-

The letter 'A' is represented as '.-'. Similarly, each alphabet has its own special signals known to Morse code trained technicians.

Let us assume that your name is HARI. We can translate it into Morse code as follows:

H = ...

A = .-

R = .-.

I = ..

HARI = ...- .-. ..

Any English word or sentence can be converted to Morse code (series of dots and dashes) by using such simple rules!

In a telegraph office, a special expert who knows this Morse code language by heart is available round the clock. When you give him a message, he converts it into Morse code either manually, or by using a special machine which helps him to do it faster.

Once this is done, a telegram equipment sends this Morse code message (dots and dashes in different combinations) as electric signals. These signals travel through wires and reach the destination quickly.

But who will read the messages at the other end? Just like the machine which sent the Morse code messages, there is another machine on the destination side to read these electric signals, convert them into human readable text and print them on a small roll of paper. Then the message is delivered to the person to whom the telegram is addressed.

Compared to letters, telegrams reached people faster but cost more. Therefore, people used it only when there was an emergency or send messages and wishes on special events.

Now, this is a book about mobile phones. Why are we discussing about telegrams in detail?

The reason is that telegraph technology is the forefather of telephone technology. Without telegrams, we would have never got our phones or mobiles.

After phones established a wide reach, many people have stopped using telegrams. A whole new generation of young people like you may not even understand what a telegram means.

But we must thank Mr. Morse and his telegraph technology for our telephones today!

First Leap

When the telegram was introduced, the general public was astonished. People were unable to believe that a message can reach its destination in a matter of hours, rather than days or weeks.

Soon, people accepted telegrams as a way of life and started using it whenever necessary. Both individuals and corporations benefited a lot from it.

This set the scientists thinking. They started discussing, 'What's next? Can we better this technology? Can we do something different using these cables?'

The thought process in this direction led to an obvious question: Telegram is the science of transmitting alphabets, words and sentences in the form of electric signals through a cable. Similarly, can we transmit human voices also? It was a strange, wild dream. But eventually, it led to the invention of telephones!

By the way, do you know who invented the telephone? That's easy, it was Alexander Graham Bell. The information is available in every General Knowledge book!

Guess what...This is only a half-truth. Graham Bell is not the sole brain behind the telephone. He is just one of the many inventors who made this wonder machine possible.

Even today, there is confusion about who really invented telephones. Some claim Alexander Graham Bell was the first scientist to come up with a working model of telephone. But many disagree and point to other inventors.

The confusion is understandable. Because, in those days many scientists and hobbyists attempted at inventing telephone-like gadgets. Most of them failed, few tasted partial success, and only a handful went through that last mile and was able to show some result for all their hard work.

The people were really confused. Newspapers and magazines published raving articles about different inventions that looked like telephones. But nobody was sure what worked and what didn't.

On February 14th, 1876, there was a huge commotion in New York City's Patent Office. Two scientists came forward at the same time, and claimed that they had invented a working model of the telephone. They were Alexander Graham Bell and Elisha Gray.

Let us not debate on who was first. Remember, the telephone was invented in the latter part of 19th Century. Alexander Graham Bell toiled for many months in his little laboratory before he could claim a piece of the telephone fame. But when he did, that dramatic event got etched in the history of humankind forever.

'Mister Watson' - These were the two words Alexander Graham Bell spoke on the world's first phone. At that time, his assistant Watson was in the next room. He heard Alexander's voice over phone.

It's amazing! Today we can talk to people in America, Africa, even to Antarctica, sitting in the comforts of our home. But all these started with a small telephone call from Alexander's room to Watson's room close by.

Soon, Alexander Graham Bell demonstrated his telephone to the American public. It was a pleasant surprise for them to see this innovation, and they were thrilled about its future possibilities.

For his part, Graham Bell didn't rest on his laurels. He continued his research on the telephone and made many changes and improvements to the device invented by him. Finally, he perfected this technology so that it can be mass produced and used by millions of people.

The proof of his hard work is in front of our eyes. More than 100 years have passed since Alexander Graham Bell invented the telephone. But even today, modern telephones use almost the same architecture that he had proposed a century ago. Not much has changed; Graham Bell's invention has really stood the test of time!

What is so great about the telephone architecture? How does it look like anyway? In fact, it's not that difficult. We can guess it ourselves.

Imagine Alexander Graham Bell sitting in one room, and his assistant Watson in another. If Alexander's voice has to be heard by Watson, what would they need?

First, in Alexander's room there should be a device which accepts or receives his voice. In the next room, we need another device which does the reverse. That is, replaying the voice of Alexander.

But this is not enough. We need something to connect the two devices. That is the most important part of this architecture, without which Alexander can talk but Watson can't hear anything. To summarise, they needed:

- A device to accept human voice
- A device to replay human voice
- Something to connect these two devices

Like the basic colours red, blue and green, these are the three basic components of telephone architecture. All other components are either secondary, or derived from these, and hence, less important.

Since the architecture hasn't changed much in so many years, you can use your grand father's phone even today without too much difficulty. This mixed adopting of both ancient and modern concepts is a specialty of the telephone technology.

Surprisingly, not only the land line telephones, but also mobile phones use a similar technology. Only the devices inside are slightly changed, to adopt mobile communication. Otherwise there is no big difference between those wired phones, and these modern mobile gadgets.

So, this emphasises that we need to study more carefully what Alexander Graham Bell and his followers did. It will give us an insight into the working of the basic telephones, how they changed in the later days and how scientists were able to adopt those emerging technologies into tiny mobile devices. In fact, the same analysis may even give a clue on what's in store for us in future.

Let's get started!

Mikes and Speakers

It's Yesudas's music concert today, and we couldn't get tickets for the front row. All our seats are at the back of the huge auditorium. Of course, we are a little disappointed, but don't worry, we will still be able to hear his voice clearly, even from this great distance. How is that possible?

In front of the singer, you can see one or more mikes. In the earlier days, most of the mikes were connected through wires. But today's modern mikes are wireless. So, what does the mike do?

Mike is a device that converts human voice, sound from music instruments or, any other noise into electric signals. In this case, the singer's voice is converted into the corresponding electric signals by the mikes positioned in front of him.

Similarly, there is another device on the audience's side. This is called a speaker. Depending on the size of the room and the number of people in the audience, we may have one or more speakers across the area. These speakers may be movable or attached permanently to the walls or other fixtures in the auditorium.

But why do we need so many speakers? What is the function of a speaker?

A speaker does the opposite of what a mike does – it converts electrical signals into sound. Thus it magnifies a human voice, or music from an instrument. This is called amplification. It involves the technique of increasing the quality of sound to a higher level so that many people can listen to it and enjoy the programme.

In addition to mikes and speakers, there are wires connecting the two. Sound travels through these wires and reaches our ears. We can understand them better if we bring these three concepts to telephony.

Let us assume that the singer of today's concert becomes a good friend of yours. One fine morning, you feel like listening to his sweet melodies. Immediately, you pickup the phone, dial the singer's number and ask, 'Sir, can you please sing something for me?'

It's a strange request. But he understands, and starts singing immediately. You could hear his honey-soaked voice through your telephone. Wait a minute. There is something wrong here!

Earlier, when he sang in the concert, he had a mike in front of him, and many speakers around, connected to each other by wires. So we could hear his voice even though we were far away.

But in this case, we are far away but we are able to listen to his voice clearly. So, could there be a mike and a speaker in our phones? You got it right. This is the basic principle of telephone communication and it works like the music concert example, but in a larger scale.

Do you have a land line phone at home? Analyze it carefully. You can clearly see two distinct parts in it. The top of the phone has a tiny speaker. That's where we hear the voice of the person we are speaking to.

Similarly, the bottom of the phone contains a small mike, into which we speak. And it reaches the other person through the telephone lines or wires.

The same principle is applicable for mobile phones too. Even though they look very different, you can clearly notice the mike portion at the bottom and speaker portion at the top. However, they are smaller in size in the mobile phone. In fact, these are much more powerful and can capture or replay even a wee bit of sound around us.

Look at the picture below. It clearly shows the mike and speaker of a land line or a mobile phone.

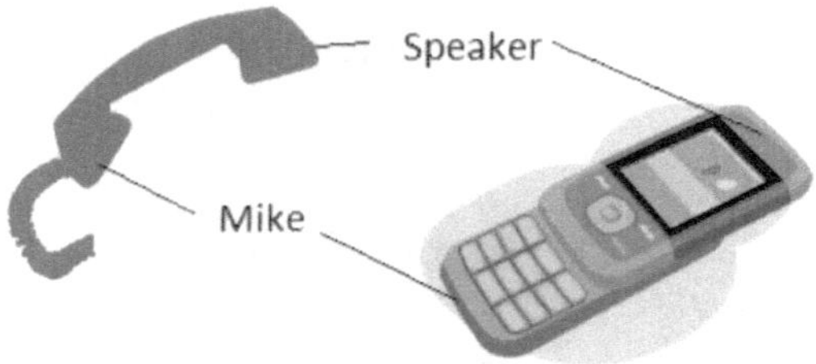

Coming back to our original discussion, when we talk to someone, we have a phone each, which means we both have one mike and one speaker with us.

Suppose you are talking to your friend. You start with a 'Hello'. When you say this, the mike portion of your phone converts your voice into electrical signals and sends them to your friend who may be sitting in another street/place/country.

At the other end, the electric signals are once again converted and replayed by the speaker in your friend's phone. Now he replies with a 'Hi, how are you'. This again gets picked up by his mike, becomes an electrical signal, travels through communication networks, reaches our phone, and gets amplified as a voice in our speaker.

In short, there are four components that work together like a perfect symphony: your phone's mike, speaker, and the mike and speaker of your friend's phone. Even if one of these fails, your communication will be incomplete.

To enable the perfect linking of these four components, there is a huge telephone network set up across the world. In the case of land line phones, the connection is made using cables. Similarly, mobile phones use transmitting towers, satellites and many other advanced technologies, which we shall discuss in detail later.

There is one question pending – when our voice gets converted to electrical signals, how does it travel through the cables? And how does it become a human voice again at the other end?

Vibrations

Every day, our world is becoming dirtier. From our roads to the air we inhale, everything is being polluted heavily.

You might have noticed that many people riding a two-wheeler now wear a handkerchief or a face mask to close their nose and mouth. This acts as a filter to prevent unnecessary particles entering our lungs.

Let us say you and I are travelling in a bike, wearing such handkerchief masks. Suddenly, a voice is heard: 'What's the time?' You know for sure it was my voice.

But my mouth is covered by a cloth. Still, you are able to recognise my voice, and answer my question. How? This is because, when I speak, air comes out of my mouth and it moves the handkerchief slightly. From this you know I am talking. In fact, if you pay more attention, you can even read my lips and understand the words, though you are not able to hear them.

This looks like a trick. Let somebody talk, and we will provide a small, thin piece of cloth or plate in front of them, which would capture their voice as vibrations. By listening to those vibrations, you can understand what they are talking.

Ancient telephones used the same trick. Their mikes had a metal plate which vibrated depending on the voice spoken into it. When I say vibrations, don't imagine huge earthquake kind of movements. As the plate is small, it will only have tiny vibrations.

But the point is, if you speak softly, the plate will have mild vibrations. Instead, if someone shouts, it will produce bigger vibrations. These changes are monitored by a special device in the mike area and converted into electric signals accordingly.

For example, when you say 'Hello Dad, How are you?' on the telephone, depending on your voice, and change of pitch, lots of electrical signals are created. These would be an exact match to what you just said.

But, why are we doing this? Sending human voice over telephone cables is not easy. But when we convert them into corresponding electrical signals, they can be sent to far away places without any difficulty.

Now, imagine that your father, who's sitting elsewhere, is eager to listen to your voice. Whatever you spoke a few microseconds earlier has been converted into electrical signals, sent over cables and to reach his phone. They get converted into vibrations and are played back in his phone's speaker area.

This is just a reverse of what happened earlier. Therefore, we can summarise as follows:

- When we speak, the speech creates vibrations in our phone's mike. They get converted into electrical signals.
- These signals are transmitted to the destination area through cables.
- In the destination phone, the signals get converted into vibrations, which play back as a human voice.
- When someone answers the phone, the whole process takes place in reverse.

Ah, this sounds like a lot. But today's telephones are very intelligent and do these things automatically, so that the users need not worry or understand the underlying technology. This is what has made telephones a widespread phenomenon across the world. It is now within the reach of even illiterate people, unlike any other major technology.

Whatever we discussed till now applies to both landline phones and mobiles. Except for the use of some devices, there are not many changes in mobile telephony. We are going to discuss this in detail in the forthcoming chapters.

The complexity is that there are hundreds, thousands and millions of phones all over the world. How can we possibly link all of them?

Let's do a mental calculation. In a city, only two people have telephones. So we need only one connection between these two and they can talk to each other at anytime.

But few days later, another person buys a telephone. So there are three people with a telephone now. We need three connections between them: A to B, B to C and C to A.

Imagine a fourth telephone. The number of connections jumps to six: A to B, B to C, C to D, D to A, B to D and A to C. What about five? We would need 10 connections.

For six? We need 15 connections. Seven? 21 connections. 50 phones? 1225 connections. 100 phones? 4950 Connections!

Do you see the problem? When we have crores of phones across the globe, the number of connections we need would grow exponentially. It is practically impossible to build and maintain such a huge number of connections.

Earlier, when the number of telephones in this world was minimal, real people did the job of connecting the phones manually. They were called 'telephone operators'. Whenever you wanted to talk to someone, you had to call the operator first, who would ask for your destination number and connect you.

Later, technology removed this unnecessary human effort and made everything automatic. Today, all telephone exchanges are digital and we can reach anyone anywhere without the involvement of an intermediate person.

If you are in Chennai and want to call your friend in Goa, the call goes from your home to the local telephone exchange and connects you to the Goa exchange. From there you get connected to your friend. This forms a private network between the two of you, and you can talk without any interruption.

Cell phone

When basic telephony became this easy, technologists started thinking ahead, 'Why not a wireless phone?'

Collection of cells

Some people call them cell phones, while others call them mobile phones. What's the correct word? Both are correct. But the key is in the word cell, which we need to understand better.

A mobile phone has a battery cell in it. Is that the reason we call it a cell phone? No. That's silly; because the word 'cell' means a totally different thing here.

Mobile phone communication is much more complex than the regular landline network. This is because the person carrying the mobile phone can be in any corner of the globe. There has to be a foolproof way of locating the person easily, quickly and reliably. To achieve this, the entire world is split into many small areas called 'cells'.

Cell diagram

Let us say your house is in the middle of a city. You are sitting in the drawing room on a sofa, watching television. Suddenly, your mobile phone begins to sing a melody indicating that there is an incoming call. You immediately pick up the phone. Your best friend Arjun is on the other side, and both of you start chatting.

If you look carefully at a cell phone tower, you will notice that it has three antennae each looking in a different direction. Each antenna serves a different cell. In turn, each cell is surrounded by three towers and so it is served by three antennae (see Figure below). Each of the three towers receives Arjun's call, but it is that one which gets the strongest signal that processes his call.

During the call, you feel hungry. You walk to the

kitchen, pick some snacks and return to your favourite sofa, continuing the conversation all the while.

Guess what? You have moved from one cell to another, and returned to the original cell. But you were not aware of it because your mobile phone seamlessly switched between these cells ensuring that your conversation is not interrupted.

As you move around within a cell with your phone switched on, the phone listens for a control signal from the towers around. If it does not detect any signal from any of the towers, it gives the caller a message that you are out of range. If a signal is received, the phone monitors the strength of the signal and selects the tower nearest to you.

If you move out of one cell into an adjacent one, then a base station in the adjacent cell takes over. It sounds like magic. But millions of mobile phones are performing this wizardry every minute, every second. They make sure that people like you and me can move between rooms, streets, cities, states, even across countries without knowing about it. A mobile phone is also called a cell phone because it moves between cells routinely and keeps the communication alive.

If you want to call a friend in Delhi, all you need to do is pick up the phone, dial (or search) his number, and his phone starts ringing immediately. The moment he picks it up, there is an imaginary wire created between you and your friend, through which you can converse without any disturbances. You can both hear each others' voices clearly irrespective of where you live.

It looks very simple and obvious. But the truth is, thousands of scientists have worked for so many years to make such a network possible. Compared to the effort put in to invent a wired telephone, they had to work doubly hard to cut the unnecessary wires.

To understand this further, let us use a simple mobile phone. It is very small but has all the features that a bigger telephone had earlier, and also has additional features which were never thought of before.

This is the first challenge in mobile telephony. How do we make a device so small that it can be carried around everywhere, and yet pack it with very powerful features, to take care of all the modern requirements?

Remember, just making a phone small and powerful is not enough. It needs to have the ability to enable a person call anybody from anywhere. Similarly, when we travel, we should be able to pick incoming calls, irrespective of where we are at that moment. If these two facilities are missing, a mobile phone will be nothing but an empty box.

From this point of view, a mobile phone is nothing but a small radio. You heard it right! We have listened to FM radio on our mobile phones. But the phone itself is a very private radio. Isn't it surprising?

A Private Radio

Do you know how the radio works? There are radio stations around the world. This is where news items, music concerts, drama and many other interesting programmes are recorded. They are later converted to electromagnetic waves, and broadcast using special devices called 'transmitters'.

These waves are accepted by little radio sets in our homes. As they receive radio waves and play them for us, we call them 'receivers'.

In our country, there are hundreds of radio stations – in Delhi, Mumbai, Bengaluru, Chennai and many other smaller cities. These stations transmit radio waves which are received and played back by millions of receivers across India.

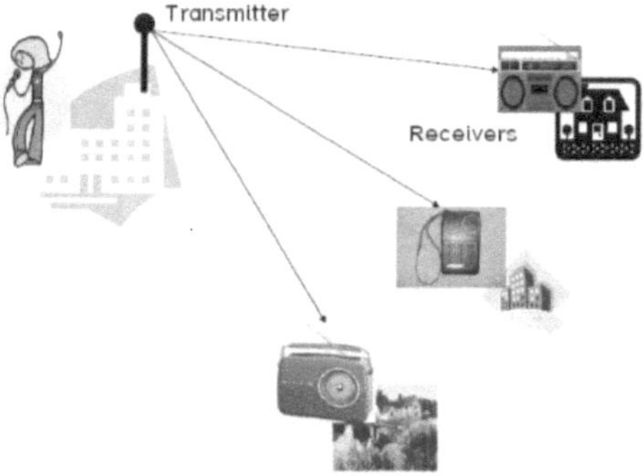

For a change, assume that there is a special device which has both the transmitter and receiver in it. What can you do with it? First of all, because the device contains a transmitter, we can speak into it and convert our voice to radio signals, and broadcast them. It contains a receiver too, so it can accept radio signals meant for us, and play them back.

You got the idea. That's precisely what our mobile phone does! Radha and Geetha are thick friends. Both of them have the latest mobile phones.

Radha is in a railway station as she is travelling to her native place. Her friend Geetha is in a super market, picking apples. Suddenly, Geetha has a doubt. She wants to speak to Radha immediately. So, she searches for her mobile phone, and dials her friend's number. At the railway station, Radha's mobile starts ringing. She picks it up and starts talking, 'Hi Geetha, How are you?'

What does this actually mean? 'Radha Broadcasting Corporation' (RBC in short) transmits a message 'Hi Geetha, How are you?' This reaches Geetha's receiver and she could listen to her friend's voice, just like you enjoy a radio programme.

Geetha responds, 'I am fine Radha, How are you doing?' Now GBC (Geetha Broadcasting Corporation)'s transmitter sends this short programme (message) into the air. Radha's mobile phone receives it and plays it back to her.

Such a 'radio-like' communication happens whenever we talk on a mobile phone. Each one of our mobile phones acts as a private radio station, and also a receiver.

Remember, there is one important difference between the regular radio and the mobile phone. In case of ordinary radio transmission, one person will do the talking (broadcasting) and many others would listen in to it. But these people can't reply or respond as they don't have transmitters of their own. It's called a one-way communication.

On the contrary, mobile phones have both transmitter and receiver. So the loop is closed and our communication becomes two-way. It is as if you can ask questions to a speaker on the radio, and get your responses or clarifications immediately.

Another difference is that compared to radio transmission, mobile communication is very personal. Two people can broadcast their thoughts and receive others' thoughts at the same time. But others can't listen to what they are talking (unless and until they eavesdrop, which is very nasty!)

Other than these two factors (two-way, personal communication), a mobile phone acts pretty much like a radio. Even the underlying technology (hardware) of a mobile phone is very similar to radio transmitters and receivers.

We have already seen in detail, what's inside a telephone. The same mike-speaker pair is present here also. Using this, our mobile phone converts the speech into waves, or receives and plays them for us.

But we need a third component, to make a telephone communication complete. It is the connection between various mobile devices. Let us focus on that next!

Towering Achievement

Today's mobile phones are much more than simple communication devices. They have become style statements and an indicator of how wealthy and modern you are.

But even when you spend thousands of rupees on a mobile phone, there is no guarantee that it would work anywhere, anytime. The phone may have a camera, audio player, video player, timer, alarm clock and many other features, but its basic functionality is to call someone or receive calls from them. If these don't happen, the phone is of no real value.

What makes a mobile phone tick? It's the mobile communication network. This network is the most important part in mobile telephony. It gives us the power to call any phone around the world. In the past, we had the concept of Trunk Call. If you want to talk to somebody in a faraway city, first you had to book a trunk call with the operator. After a few minutes, they would connect you to the requested number, making the telephone conversation possible.

These days, nobody books a trunk call because this technology has improved, and we can automatically get connected to any number, local or long distance.

When it comes to landline phones, making this connection is comparatively easy. Whether it is manual or automatic, you have wires that tie every phone. This means we would always know where a particular phone is.

On the other hand, mobile phones are truly wire-less. They are not tied to any particular place. I may be sitting at home, or in the school, or in my dad's office, or walking on a road, or playing cricket with my friends, or sleeping in my garden hammock. Wherever I am, others should be able to reach me on my mobile phone. That's a very interesting challenge.

To enable such a dynamic network, mobile phone technology uses the concept of cells. Wherever we need mobile network, small cells are formed so that we are constantly inside a cell.

Sometimes, especially when you are travelling or visiting a very small village, your phone may display, 'No signal'. This means there is no coverage, and we are not inside any cell.

Other than such rare situations, we can be assured that we will always be in a cell and our mobile phone would know that. It connects to the nearest tower, enabling us to make or receive calls.

As we saw earlier, voice communication between two people on the mobile phone takes place through radio waves. A limited number of frequencies are allotted to each cell for this purpose. When Geetha talks to Radha, her voice is carried to the base station on one frequency while Radha's reply comes back on a different frequency. In effect, this even lets them both to speak at the same time. The two frequencies together make up a channel. As soon as Geetha's cell phone selects the tower closest to her, the tower allots a channel that is free, to start a conversation with Radha.

Now that a channel is alloted, how does voice travel. The base station tower that receives the voice from Geetha's cell phone is sent to a base station controller in her city. A base station controller is part of a base station subsystem and services a number of base station towers. The base station subsystem consists of several base station controllers. The call from Geetha is received by a base station controller and redirected on to a Mobile Telephone Switching Office or MTSO. This is also sometimes referred to as Mobile Services Switching Centre or MSC.

One of the tasks of the MTSO is to keep track of the location of all the cell phones in the network at any point in time. Every cell phone that is switched on keeps checking for the control signal from a tower nearby. This helps the tower identify the location of the cell phone and the information is sent on to the MTSO through the base station controller.

Picture from magazine

Such information is collected from all the base station controllers and stored in a data base at the MTSO. When Geetha's call reaches the MTSO, it searches the data base and traces Radha's location and forwards Geetha's call to her. The MTSOs also have a radio link with land line exchanges, so there is no problem if Radha's number is a land line.

When we speak to someone on the cell phone, we may be tempted to consider it as very simple and easy. But, the whole sequence of operations as described above is completed in very little time.

What if we are walking? Or running? Or travelling in a moving vehicle? Don't worry. The mobile phone is intelligent enough to know when you are moving from one cell to another, and switches to the new tower. The best part is that this change doesn't interrupt our conversation.

It is good to remember that all this has become possible only because of the great advances in designing computer chips to carry out the complex operations in fractions of a second. This seemingly simple solution was not invented by a single person. It evolved step by step, over years of hard work by many scientists and innovators!

To summarise, the mobile phone in your hand works with the nearest network available at any given point of time and that's what makes your phone truly mobile.

Wire-less Wonder

When (and why) did phones become wire-less? Any gadget, when it comes to the market, is seen by its users with awe. They think it's the best, and no further improvements are required.

But slowly, when they start using it on a regular basis, they ask questions like, 'Hey, won't it be nice if this feature is available?' or 'Will it not work better with a small change?' This is when a product evolves and reaches the next stage. In that process, it may change its size, shape, usage and more.

When (wired) telephone became a big hit, both individuals and companies started using it widely. They felt an additional need for a very important feature in telephones: mobility, flexibility to carry our phone anywhere we go.

For example, if a policeman is on the road on a very important safety mission, he may want to be in touch with his superiors conveying important messages. Similarly, his boss may need to contact him on a regular basis to get updates.

This was very difficult with a phone tied to wires. People on the field had to search for the nearest phone and companies found it increasingly troublesome to contact people when necessary.

This thought process led to an important discovery: a wire-less gadget that could be carried around by people and used for internal communication. This was a must for people like policemen, army officers, firefighters and other such professionals, and could save many lives.

These wireless phones are the great, great grandfathers of today's mobile gadgets. In 1902, an American farmer Nathan B. Stubblefield invented one such device and got the patent for it.

But Nathan's prototype was very basic. Many other scientists and innovators joined the bandwagon and improved his design, and made it more reliable and usable. People started calling them radio phones.

So we need to thank the Army and police forces. They are the ones who had the broad vision to think ahead and ask for many mobile features in a wireless phone, making it a model for the future.

Even now, you can see these wireless devices in some police cars. Recently, call taxi service providers have also started using similar devices. Compared to modern phones, these are noisy but work perfectly well, and are comparatively cheaper too!

The Second World War took place in the middle of the 20th Century. Wireless technology was heavily used in this war for effective communication between the fighting troops and their headquarters.

After the war, telephone and communication experts started discussing seriously about the possibilities of making wire-less technology accessible to the general public. It's not as easy as you think. A city may have only a few hundreds of policemen. Setting up a radio phone (wireless) network between the limited people's network is relatively simple.

But when it comes to the general public, there will be thousands, or tens of thousands of people. Big cities may have millions. Also, they will be spread out in different areas, they may even move out of their home town. Will the wireless technology cope up with such drastic changes on a continuous basis?

Companies manufacturing electronic devices were worried. Still, they knew that such a generic mobile device would have many takers, and it would sell like hot cakes. As they realised there was money for the grabs, they rolled-up their sleeves and started research on a mass-production mobile telephone.

To tell the truth, not many of them succeeded. They were able to make small advancements, but when field tests were conducted, they were not able to manage most of their products. A few devices which worked were very heavy, and carrying them was a pain.

Fortunately for us, scientists didn't lose focus or hope. They continued to innovate smaller, more powerful, more reliable devices. Failures didn't stop them from trying hard, again and again.

In 1981, the world's first mobile telephone network called the NMT (Nordic Mobile Telephony Network) was formed in Scandinavia. This included many European/Nordic countries such as Denmark, Finland, Iceland, Norway, Sweden and others.

The formation of NMT is considered an important turning point in the history of mobile telephones. Why? This group tried to standardise many technologies and solutions for designing and using mobile phones.

For example, on what basis do we split the areas which need a mobile network? How can we make sure two people talking over the mobile network are not interrupted by other similar connections? How frequently should we bill the customers? When they move from one place to another, how to ensure continuous (roaming) connectivity?

These questions sound very silly to us because we know the answers to all of them today. But in those days, when the mobile telephone was in its infancy, people were unclear as to how different things would work, and NMT provided some decent explanations. It was a welcome change in this direction.

Compared to today's mobile standards, NMT was relatively small, and was left with more questions than answers. But people were very impressed by its activities, and many companies wanted to join the mobile revolution.

Soon, the news spread to other countries, and they also started creating similar mobile networks making the best use of the available technology framework. After all, it's easier to copy somebody than create it from the scratch.

This 'copy cat' mentality led to the introduction of several NMT kinds of standards in many other developed nations. All the stakeholders (mobile service providers, device manufacturers and general public) welcomed such measures because it brought some discipline in this relatively young field.

NMT was well ahead of its time. It provided very good coverage, seamless roaming facility and many other advanced features.

Still, people were not ready to buy a mobile phone. Service providers had to do something very innovative (and drastic) to attract users!

Is it a Brick? Is it a Phone?

Recently, scientists conducted a curious experiment to find how much we value 'free' offers. They did so with two brands of chocolates. The high quality chocolate was priced at 5 rupees, and the other one at 2 rupees.

Buyers naturally preferred quality products. So the 5-rupee chocolate sold 60%, and the 2-rupee (lower quality) chocolate sold only 40%.

Next day, they reduced the price of both chocolates by 2 rupees – the first one came down to 3 rupees, and the second chocolate cost zero rupees. In other words, it was given away for free.

Technically speaking, this shouldn't affect people's purchase pattern. After all, the prices of both the chocolates prices were reduced by the same amount (2 rupees). Therefore, people should prefer the high quality chocolate at purchase rate of 60% as against the other chocolate at 40%.

But people reacted totally different now. They opted for the free chocolate 90% of the time. Only 10% of the consumers bought the other (high quality) chocolate.

That's the power of the word 'free'. No wonder every product manufacturer and shop owner gives something or the other 'free' to attract buyers. They know people jump at a free offer, compared to any other (even better) deal.

The same was true in case of mobile phones also. Even though these phones were very useful, people hesitated to buy them because it was overpriced, or the calls were very expensive.

In fact, those days, people had to pay for both outgoing and incoming calls and were frustrated. After all, on a land line phone, no one pays for the incoming calls. Why on a mobile phone should anyone pay for even the calls one receives?

Technically speaking, on a mobile network, the person making the call and the one who receives it are using the infrastructure equally. So, companies had to charge both of them, if they had to stay profitable.

But the public didn't accept it. This made mobile phone adoption painfully slow. Sometimes, it looked as if the world had simply rejected this wonder product.

That's when NMT intervened and made a strong statement, 'Just like any other phone, people shouldn't be charged for incoming calls on the mobile. It should be given to them as free'.

Ah, there was the 'free' word! You know what would have happened next. All of a sudden, people started thinking of mobile phones as a necessity. Even those who were strongly advocating against its use now felt they needed one.

Mobile phones those days were large, very large. Sometimes, people were genuinely confused, 'Am I carrying a phone? Or a brick?' But irrespective of size, many loved mobile phones, especially businessmen. They felt mobile phone would give them a flood of new opportunities as they can be reached anytime, anywhere.

Because of such support, NMT was slowly becoming a global standard for mobile telecommunication. Companies like Nokia/Mobira, Philips and Ericsson came up with innovative models of mobiles at a faster rate. These phones had better performance and cost much less compared to the earlier models.

In 1982, Mobira introduced its first mobile phone 'Mobira Senator.' It was slightly bigger than a brick, and had a small handle on top, to help being carried around. But why do we need a handle for a mobile phone? That's because, Mobira Senator weighed 9.8 kilograms!

Mobira Senator (1982)

Wait a minute. How can people carry a 10-kg mobile phone? Wouldn't it break their legs if they dropped it by mistake? True. That's why first generation mobile phones were developed as car phones. They were fixed in cars as a permanent gadget. As cars could move around the city, they were truly mobile, reaching wherever people went.

Like its weight, the phone cost a fortune. Only a select few could afford such a mobile phone. Soon, this norm changed. Innovators came up with advanced microchips and smaller batteries which could be mass produced at a cheaper rate. This made phones compact, and more affordable.

Still, it hadn't reached everybody yet, especially the middle class. Something had to be done!

Cityman & Gorbachev

April 9, 1987. The Soviet Union's then president Mikhail Sergeyevich Gorbachev was visiting the Nokia factory. Everyone was thrilled and last minute arrangements were in full swing, to make this visit a memorable one.

Just a few weeks earlier, Nokia had introduced a new mobile phone called Cityman. It was the world's first true mobile phone, because people could carry it wherever they went.

While the technical people in Nokia were excited about Cityman, their sales force was worried, 'Of course, our product is great. But will people shell out money and buy it?'

They tried really hard and advertised Cityman everywhere. Nokia made sure that people were aware of this product's unique features and tried to persuade them to go for one.

All these hard selling techniques helped only initially. Cityman (and other Nokia mobile phones) sold in good numbers. Still, there were millions of others who could afford a mobile phone, but were not buying one.

Nokia wanted to do something to increase people's awareness of mobile phones. All they needed was a small gimmick that would make people look up and take notice.

Nokia decided to use Gorbachev's visit to their advantage. They planned to give Gorbachev a phone, make him call somebody from it, take a photograph of the same and publish it in every newspaper. Wouldn't that be wonderful?

On the specific day, President Gorbachev came as planned. Executives welcomed him with a cute 'Nokia Cityman' Mobile.

A confused Gorbachev asked, 'What is this?'

'It's our newest product, why don't you try it once?'

Gorbachev was thrilled. He dialled a number, and started talking. Cameras flashed.

That was the biggest turning point in the history of mobile phones. That small phone conversation made mobile phones so popular that everybody took notice of it. It gave Nokia a lot of free publicity, and the general concept of mobile phone itself became a 'cool' thing!

Five Generations

There are five distinct stages in the development of mobile telephone technology. In each of these steps, there were wonderful innovations which made the progress swift. In the past 25 years, there is no other technology which has grown this much, this fast.

Each of these five stages in mobile telephony is called a 'Generation'. Accordingly, they are codenamed as 0G, 1G, 2G, 3G and 4G.

'0G' means, Generation Number 0. Ancient mobile phones used during and immediately after Second World War come under this stage. These phones had very limited features, and reliability was a big concern.

In '0G' phones, there was no assurance that you would always be connected. There was no centralised organisation to provide standards. Each manufacturing company followed its own norms and people found it very difficult.

Next, NMT happened (1981). Many companies adopted their products to suit the standards suggested by this organisation. These were the real 'first generation' (1G) phones.

Compared to '0G' phones, the '1G' phones had many new facilities, most of them automated. Telephone conversations became less painful and more reliable. There was a very strict quality and standardisation control, which many countries followed to ensure customer satisfaction and acceptance.

Still very few people bought '1G' phones – weight and cost was a huge factor. There were few other missing links, which many pointed out. Everyone wanted these rectified, so that mobile phones would look (and work) much better.

That's how '2G' phones came into the picture. These used digital technology for superior speed and clarity. 'Digital' means converting anything to a series of digits - 0s and 1s. This kind of digitised data can be easily stored, transmitted, encoded and decoded, making it a very flexible data handling mechanism.

Before digital technology was introduced, most of the mobile telephony devices were using Analog systems. Slowly, from mobile (handheld) devices to network equipments, everything moved to digital, reducing errors and improving performance.

So when you talked over a mobile phone, your voice would be converted to the corresponding digital format, and be transmitted using the 2G phone equipments. Finally, they would be received and converted back to voice, all with digital technology.

One major change digital technology brought was clarity - 1G mobile phones always had the problem of external noise. Even in short distance calls, you had to concentrate hard to listen and understand what the other person said.

This drastically changed in 2G Phones. They had superb voice quality, you felt as if both the persons communicating were standing in the same room and conversing. In India, most of the devices and telephone network equipments used are 2G.

2G phones were small in size. This was possible because of the advancements in battery technology. Small batteries came cheap, but lasted longer. 2G phones came with another innovative feature called SMS (Short Messaging Service). This was the first major non-voice application for mobile phones, and people simply loved it.

Today, we can't even dream of a mobile phone without a SMS feature. People send even birthday wishes, marriage invitations, and other important messages using SMS.

These were some of the visible changes that 2G brought. There were many other invisible enhancements too. Mainly, it was possible to send more voice calls using the same bandwidth available. As more calls travelled in a smaller space, the overall cost came down, making the end users very happy!

Due to the above reasons, many mobile-based companies started focusing on digital technology. Everyday, new mobile phones were being introduced. Even the communication devices became digital so that both voice and data could be sent at the same time.

To browse the internet, you do not need a computer anymore. As 2G mobile phones can handle data transfer, you can visit websites, send Email, multimedia messages, book train, bus, flight tickets and do much more from your phone.

Compared to 0G and 1G, 2G technology was superb. But scientists didn't stop at this. They started thinking ahead and invented new gadgets, which became part of the third generation (3G) technology.

We don't have 3G among us yet. Only a select few countries are enjoying it today. But soon, it will take the whole world by storm. So it is very important we understand it!

Three Cheers to 3G

Have you used a latest version of mobile phone recently? Did you notice anything different?

No. The phone looks the same as before. What's new?

These days, mobile phones are undergoing technical advancements. There are some very exciting innovations taking place but we can't see or feel any of those. As the old saying goes, 'change is in the air!'

To understand this better, we need to take another look at the underlying technology behind mobile phones. As we saw earlier, mobile phones are nothing but small radios. When you call someone on a mobile phone an invisible network (of radio waves) is established between your phone and theirs. This acts as the communication vehicle between the two of you.

But we don't make full use of this vehicle. In the middle of our conversation we pause so many times and it goes unused. Just imagine the huge wastage of bandwidth when millions of people like us misuse the communication infrastructure like this.

To solve this problem, technologists have introduced some innovative concepts in mobile networking and bandwidth sharing. These form the basis for 3G (Third generation) mobile framework.

Compared to the earlier 1G (Analog Cellular Technology) and 2G (Digital Cellular Technology) networks, 3G is much more superior in terms of effective and efficient bandwidth utilisation. Therefore, 3G phones have many functions other than just plain talking.

For example, on a 3G network, you can browse internet at very high speed. Live cricket matches can be telecast and watched on the phone. Superb and Seamless audio, video transfer is possible because of the increased bandwidth. Starting from personal finance to office work, everything a computer does today is possible using 3G phones.

Take a look at this simple statistics: In a 2G network, the maximum transfer speed you can achieve is 144 kilobytes per second (KBPS). In other words, a video download may take five minutes. This is slow, but manageable. Right?

Enter 3G. This network can provide you a speed of up to 2 or 3 megabytes per second (MBPS) – the same video gets downloaded in 10 seconds.

Five minutes to 10 seconds is a huge improvement indeed. No wonder these are called 'Smart Phones'!

All these sound great. But there is something wrong - why isn't everybody moving to 3G? Why only a handful of countries are using it today?

It is because setting up 3G network is not an easy task. Starting from huge towers and other infrastructure construction, regular maintenance to costs involved, everything is BIG. Not many countries can afford it.

The first few countries to understand the significance of 3G were Japan and Korea. They immediately got into action and converted their existing mobile networks to 3G. This changed the mobile scene in these countries completely, and many people started using phones for most of their everyday tasks, introducing new business opportunities and growth possibilities.

Slowly, other countries are beginning to look at them enviously, and are also catching on. In India, 3G has just been introduced, and is not available in many cities yet.

But very soon, we can expect to see its benefits all around us. Once this becomes popular and extends to the important places, 3G special smart phones like iPhone, Android and others will become commonplace.

Can smart phones make us smarter? That's a million dollar question!

GSM Vs. CDMA

Whenever people want to buy a new phone connection, they have a very big confusion, 'Should I go for GSM or CDMA?'

In fact, there is a big debate going on around the world, whether GSM is better than CDMA, or is it the other way round. Let's not worry about this, and just concentrate more on understanding both the technologies.

First of all, what are GSM and CDMA? What is the difference between these two? Why do we need two technologies, can't we manage with one?

Both GSM and CDMA are two different technologies used to create a mobile network. Technically speaking, both do the same job, but use different methods.

Before these two were introduced, there was an ancient technology called 'FDMA'. If we understand this first, we can easily grasp the GSM and CDMA concepts.

'FDMA' expands to 'Frequency Division Multiple Access'. This was an analog technology used much before the digital wave came around.

To explain FDMA, let us take a small example. A city has three schools.

Every morning, the students should start from their homes and go to school. Similarly, they should return home safely in the evening. For this, each school has built a special, exclusive road, used only by its students. For example, students of School A will use the first road, and students of School B and C will use the second and third roads respectively.

There won't be any confusion now as there are three separate roads for the three schools. Students of one school will not (and need not) enter another school's road.

This was how FDMA technology worked. Think of mobile phone users as students and telephone frequencies as the roads. Assume three people in a city (X, Y and Z) are calling their friends in another city. Each one of them is given a dedicated frequency for this purpose. Neither will anyone else interrupt this frequency nor will this frequency interfere with others' frequencies.

That's wonderful. But this has a problem too. It can work well with a small network but can't handle big volumes. Think of a city having three hundred mobile users, or three thousand, or three million—assigning dedicated frequencies for all those using analog technology was impossible.

Like other problems, this was also solved by digital technology. And that's when GSM and CDMA shot to the limelight.

GSM means 'Global System for Mobile Communication'. As the name suggests, it's used by more than 70% of mobile users across the globe. Compared to FDMA, GSM technology works very efficiently. Let us go back to our 'three schools' example to understand how GSM achieved this.

Unlike FDMA, GSM doesn't ask for three separate roads. With one road, it manages the students' traffic from all the three schools, by using a time-sharing mechanism. For example, the first school will start at 8 a.m. Its students will use the single road available between 7:45 a.m. and 8 a.m. The second school starts at 8:30 a.m., so its students won't use the road until 8:15 a.m.

Similarly, the third school starts at 9 a.m. Its students will use the road between 8:45 a.m. and 9 a.m. only.

So in the GSM model, the three schools have different timings, and manage the available single road very efficiently. This way, it saves lot of money and effort for everyone, by avoiding the second and third roads altogether.

Technically speaking, GSM allows many users to share the same mobile communication frequency, but manages their conversations internally using 'time sharing' technology, like the 'road sharing' example we just saw. But that's not convincing. If A talks to B and C talks to D, using the same frequencies, won't there be a confusion?

No. GSM has the accuracy of a microsecond, and can manage multiple conversations sharing the same frequency. Therefore, many people can use the mobile service in the available bandwidth.

Now, let's move on to CDMA or 'Code Division Multiple Access' networks. This is very different from GSM in many ways. Again, let us use the same three schools and the hundreds of students.

CDMA asks a very different question here: 'Why restrict students to use one particular road? Let us leave the choice to them. They can choose whichever road they want to!'

But won't it be risky? How are we going to make sure they reach the right school or the correct home? No problem. Let us tie a tag around each student's neck. The tag will contain their home address and the name of their school. So there won't be any confusion in their reaching the correct school, or returning home.

This is the basis of CDMA. It uses the available mobile bandwidth to send all sorts of communications. There are no restrictions in terms of frequencies to be used by each call.

Remember, these conversations are not sent as a single box. CDMA splits them into small pockets, tags them properly using special codes, and sends them across. At the other end, they are once again merged using these codes and replayed.

CDMA is quite popular in America. Recently, other countries also started using this. In India, Tata Indicom and Reliance Mobile are providing CDMA services.

On the GSM side, we have many players – Airtel, Aircel, Vodafone, Cellone, MTS, Uninor and Tata Docomo. We can find out if a particular phone is GSM or CDMA very easily. The clue is the SIM card.

GSM phones would have a SIM (Subscriber Identification Modules) card fixed to them, which can be easily changed to another phone making it truly flexible.

SIM Card

A SIM card looks very small. But it has lot of electronic components in it. This card communicates with the nearest mobile tower and makes sure we always stay connected.

On the other hand, CDMA phones have no SIM card. Their identity is permanently attached to a particular phone and you can't change it whenever you need.

Other than this, CDMA is very powerful and can handle very fast data transfer. CDMA phones also last longer because of their superb battery life. No wonder, both GSM and CDMA have very strong supporters on their sides!

Future Mobiles

How will tomorrow's mobiles look like? Recently, there was a television advertisement that caught everyone's attention. It shows a glimpse of what might be in store for us. This futuristic ad has a man carrying a mobile. Sorry, he is not carrying it, but wearing it, like a watch.

When this person wants to call somebody, he doesn't dial any number, he just thinks about it and presto, the other person's 3D face appears on the watch dial, and starts talking. After the call is over, the other person just disappears into the watch dial.

Amazing, isn't it? Well, it is not possible to design and create such a phone with today's technology. But who knows what's in store for tomorrow? Today's innovations were thought of as pure 'science fiction' yesterday, and we have them live and working now. Similarly, this 3D phone may be a reality tomorrow.

Experts say future phones will be in a 'wear'able format. It may be like a watch, or a bangle, or like a sweatband you wear on the wrist. Hence they are called 'Wristmo'.

Similar to 'Wristmo,' there may be future phones which can be worn as a chain or necklace or belt or even as a small ring on your index finger.

The main advantage of this type of phone is that you can wear it in the morning and forget about it. There's no need to carry an additional device. And nobody can steal it from you. But if phones are designed so small, how will we see the numbers, names and other display?

No problem. Future phones will have a hidden screen, which can be pulled back whenever needed. These special screens will display video, audio, television, radio programmes, internet, email, documents and many other features.

Such phones use an advanced technology which experts term as '4G'. Already people in huge numbers are working on what is possible in these fourth generation phones and networks.

We need to wait and see what '4G' has to offer. To end this book on a happy note, let us list a couple of possibilities we can expect to see in the future phones:

- Future phones will have long-lasting batteries. You don't have to constantly worry about recharging your battery. You can talk longer, exchange more data and do much more with the same battery power.
- These phones would have automatic connectivity with other electronic devices at our home or office. For example, computers, landline phones, televisions, refrigerators, food processors and other gadgets. Imagine switching off lights, changing TV channels, or starting the washing machine using your mobile, it will be a possibility in the near future!

These are just small examples, the tip of the iceberg, if you will excuse the cliché. Our future life is going to be a lot more dependent on mobile phones. Keep your fingers crossed for the 4G Magic!

Prodigy books

Biographies

1. Abdul Kalam
2. Charles Darwin
3. Marie Curie
4. Visvesvaraya
5. Srinivasa Ramanujan
6. Newton
7. Einstein
8. Edison
9. James Watt
10. Jagdish Chandra Bose
11. Alexander Graham Bell
12. Gandhi
13. Jawaharlal Nehru
14. Nelson Mandela
15. Mother Teresa
16. Florence of Nightingale
17. Vivekananda
18. Annadurai
19. Ambedkar
20. Bhagat Sigh
21. Tipu Sultan
22. Rani of Jhansi
23. Akbar
24. Shivaji
25. Bharati
26. Rabindranath Tagore
27. Sarojini Naidu
28. Shakespeare
29. Martin Luther King
30. Alexander the Great
31. Napoleon
32. Abraham Lincoln
33. Adolf Hitler
34. Charlie Chaplin
35. Walt Disney
36. Bill Gates
37. Narayana Murthy
38. Columbus
39. Hsuan Tsang
40. Marco Polo

Classics Retold

41. Homer's Iliad
42. The Odyssey
43. The Tempest
44. Hamlet
45. The Merchant of Venice
46. The Midsummer Night's Dream
47. Twelfth Night
48. King Lear
49. Macbeth
50. Romeo and Juliet
51. Antony and Cleopatra
52. Julius Caesar
53. Black Beauty
54. Oliver Twist
55. Pride and Prejudice
56. A Tale of two Cities

Mythology

57. The Ramayana
58. The Mahabharatha
59. Avatars of Vishnu

Other Titles

60. The Universe
61. Life
62. Global Warming
63. Planet Earth
64. Tsunami
65. Hinduism
66. Dinosaurs
67. Ganga
68. Madras - Chennai
69. Exam Tips
70. Television
71. Mobile Phone
72. Brilliant Brain
73. World War II
74. The Mughals
75. Sultans to Sepoy Mutiny
76. The New 7 wonders of the World

Life Skills

77. Effective Communication
78. Creative Thinking
79. Learn to Make Decisions
80. Learn to Discover your Potential
81. How to build Interpersonal skills
82. Learn to Solve Problems
83. Learn to Understand Others
84. Learn to Deal with Emotions

www.ingramcontent.com/pod-product-compliance
Lightning Source LLC
Chambersburg PA
CBHW022201160726
48282CB00024B/283
9788184934359